Your Daily 15 Minutes of Great Joy Through Holy Communion

Your Daily 15 Minutes of Great Joy Through Holy Communion

MARVIN SPROUSE, JR. PH.D.

Copyright © 2022 by Marvin Sprouse, Jr. Ph.d.

All rights reserved. No part of this book may be reproduced in any form or by any electronic or mechanical means, including information storage and retrieval systems, without permission in writing from the author and publisher, except by reviewers, who may quote brief passages in a review.

ISBN: 978-1-959434-58-0 (Paperback Edition)
ISBN: 978-1-959434-59-7 (Hardcover Edition)
ISBN: 978-1-959434-57-3 (E-book Edition)

Book Ordering Information

The Regency Publishers, US
521 5th Ave 17th floor NY, NY10175
Phone Number: (315)537-3088 ext 1007
Email: info@theregencypublishers.com
www.theregencypublishers.com

Printed in the United States of America

Contents

Dedication iii

Chapter One The Launching Of The Great Miracle 1

Chapter Two Controversies; Protestant And Catholic 8

Chapter Three A New Image 14

Chapter Four Divine Healing 18

Chapter Five Special Intentions 23

Chapter Six Your Adversary, The Devil 28

DEDICATION

This Book is dedicated to any Believers who want and expect great intimacy with Jesus Christ through Holy Communion. This Book was written for and about you.

May you experience extraordinary joy in your union with Jesus Christ through Holy Communion.

Chapter One

The Launching Of The Great Miracle

"If we but pause for a moment to consider what takes place in this sacrament, I am sure that the thought of Christ's love for us would transform the coldness of our hearts into a fire of love and gratitude." Angella of Follana

"While His disciples keep proposing more organization - Hey let's elect officers. Establish hierarchy, set standards of professionalism. Jesus quietly picked up a towel and basin of water, and began to wash their feet." Phillip Yancey.

"Who is this woman? Everyone misses it. Our preconceived notions of the scene are so powerful, that our mind blows out the incongruity and overrides our eyes." Dan Brown

In the world-famous painting, titled THE LAST SUPPER, which is probably the most frequently displayed, and therefore the most popular painting in the history of painted works, we can clearly see the agitation being manifested by the guests at that table. The artist, Leonardo De Vinci, explained that the painting was intended to portray the behavior of those guests, only seconds after Jesus announced that one of the twelve Apostles was a traitor. One of the apostles on the right side of the table, is pointing at him and probably calling out the words, "Is it I, Lord?" Surely,

Jesus knew, that within a few minutes He would, by His action and His words, launch thousands of years of confusion and controversy among numerous members of His Church. Jesus certainly knew and fully understood the chaos which would erupt after He took action and spoke the words of the miracle He was delivering to His Church and to every believing member of that Church. The action taken and the words spoken were remarkably succinct and clear. Scripture tells us that Jesus took the bread and that He blessed it, broke it, and distributed it to the guests at that table, saying, "This is my Body. Take ye and eat, Do this in remembrance of me." Today many authorities in God's Church still argue passionately about what exactly Jesus meant by His action and His words. In the following Chapter I will attempt to describe the gross and very unfortunate misconceptions of both

Protestants and Catholics on what was said and what was intended by Jesus with His action and by His words at that Last Supper. If I am extraordinarily successful in writing these words, the words will bring clarity and understanding regarding what Jesus did, what He said and what He intended to communicate to His Church at that Supper. I promise you that, at no place in the entire Bible, from Genesis to Maps, as the late Zig Ziglar was fond of saying and nowhere in that entire sacred Book did God ever say nor imply that He transformed the bread at that Last supper into a "representation" of His Body. Jesus was the all-time most clear and accurate communicator who ever spoke a word, and Jesus said, "This is my body, take ye and eat, this is my Body. Do this in remembrance of Me." By those words Jesus invited every member of His Church to take the bread and eat it because it was His body. That is what He said, and that is precisely what He meant. Because many who heard those words failed to comprehend them, most believers have simply discounted the words spoken by The Son of God. If Jesus had intended for that bread to serve as a representation of the body of Christ, then at least once, in the entire Bible, He would have taken bread and He would have said something such as, "This is a representation of my Body, Take ye and eat." I promise you that nothing remotely like that appears any place in the entire Bible. What does appear, and what we are led by Jesus to believe, is the truth He spoke, "This is my body Take ye and eat. Do this in remembrance of Me." Most Protestants never expressed any understanding of those words of the miraculous transformation of bread and wine into the Body and Blood of Jesus

Christ Himself. That was interpreted by some to be an invitation to participate in cannibalism, which Christ would never have done, because cannibalism is sin, in so many ways, and Jesus lived a sin free life.

To simply live as if Jesus had never spoken the words transforming bread into His sacred Body, is to deny a small part of the Bible, which invalidates the entire Scripture. Denying the miraculous aspects of the transubstantiation, is to say that Jesus spoke carelessly and incorrectly thereby establishing Himself as dishonest. If the Son of God spoke dishonestly about one thing, then nothing He ever said can be trusted. Jesus not only spoke truth, He was, by definition, truth. When Jesus took bread, blessed it, broke it and distributed it. and the words He spoke were. "This is my body, take ye and eat." then we need to at least attempt to figure out what He meant, instead of simply writing off the words of Jesus and, in doing that, discounting not only His words, but His divinity.

Chapter Two

Controversies; Protestant And Catholic

"Feed my sheep. Feed my sheep." He repeated. He did not say "Feed My sheep after you check their ID." Sara Miles

"What happened, once I started distributing Communion was the truly disturbing, dreadful recognition about Christianity. You can't be a Christian by yourself." Sara Miles

Most Protestants, when they encountered the words Jesus spoke during the last supper, and they did not know what those words meant, "this is my body, take ye and eat," they simply choose to disregard them, to continue their lives as if those words had never been spoken. The dominant response to the transfiguration of the entire Protestant Religion is to move on as if they never read the words. Robert Morris say recently, that the bread became a representation of Christ's body. Because Protestants failed to comprehend what Jesus meant by his words. They chose to continue to live as if they had never heard those words. I heard the gifted Religious scholar Robert Morris say recently, "Christ transformed the bread into a representation of His Body." That is incorrect in so many ways. If Christ had wanted to transform bread into a representation of His body, then some place in the entire Bible we would read of Christ saying, "This is a representation of my Body." Trust me, reader. It is not in your Bible or in any other copy I ever saw. Jesus never said anything like that, never.

The Catholics meanwhile, recognized that something extraordinary had occurred during the Last Supper, but instead of merely accepting the fact that a world-changing miracle had occurred, they took the Biblical account of what had happened, and they sent it to the Vatican, for comment by the existing Pope. Please understand that anytime you take the word of God as recorded in the Bible and either add to or take from those words, then the Bible verses are contaminated by the babel of man, and are no longer purely God's Word. When Vatican officials began to add to the words Jesus spoke at the last supper, they changed one of the essential truths Jesus was attempting to communicate those thousands of years ago. With the words "Do this in remembrance of me," Jesus instituted a massive priesthood of practitioners, and He delivered to every one of those believers the enormous power to transform mere bread and wine miraculously into the body and blood of Christ. I recently asked Dr Jimmy Nelson, my former pastor, " When Jesus said, "Do this in remembrance of me, to whom was He talking? As he usually does, Doctor Nelson gave me a succinct and accurate answer. He replied with only two words, "His church." The words, "His Church" includes every believer and follower of Christ.

When Jesus said, "Do this in remembrance of me." He was throwing open the ability to transform ordinary Bread and Wine into the sacred Body and Blood of Jesus Christ.

When the powers that be at the Vatican examined those very simple words spoken by Jesus, they decided that **They would** simply disagree with the words of Jesus as spoken in the Bible, so they arbitrarily changed those words, by specifying that the only persons who could perform what they called the Transubstantiation, changing Bread and Wine into the actual Body and Blood of Jesus needed approval from the Vatican. They further limited their findings insisting that not only was anyone performing the transubstantiation required to be a graduate of a Catholic Seminary, but that he needed to be ordained in a lengthy ceremony of ordination performed by an official of the church holding at least the rank of Bishop. The Lutherans sought distinction from their form of Communion from the Catholic Version, so they proclaimed that the Bread and Wine were not transformed as the Catholics had stated in a transubstantiation but the Body and Blood of Christ appeared right next to the Bread and Wine in what they called a Consubstantiation. Does his sound silly to you? It does to me, but such is life whenever man attempts to rewrite the word of God.

Some crude and cruel critics of a Christian's consumption of Holy Communion, have said that to actually eat the Body and Blood of anyone, even of Jesus, in Holy Communion, is nothing but cannibalism. I will present a very different image of Holy Communion In the next chapter.

Chapter Three

A New Image

"The only thing worse than being blind is having sight but no vision," Helen Kellar

"Vision is the art of seeing what is invisible to others." Jonathan Swift

"Just because a man loses the use of his eyes, doesn't mean he lacks vision." Stevie Wonder

Over a decade ago someone at the Walt Disney Organization came up with a new word, "Imagineering." That word contains the syllable, "neering" suggesting some type of commerce such as engineering or astronomy. The first syllable of the word, "Imagine" suggests that people could and should be using their imagination in their work, just as they use their brains and their brawn. I have already written about how man failed to receive the meaning Christ intended when He instituted Holy Communion. Man failed to comprehend what Jesus meant when he took ordinary bread and said, "This is my Body, take ye and eat," and when He took wine and pronounced, "This is my blood, take ye and drink," because man failed to realize that Jesus was speaking both literally and spiritually. The traditional image of man eating meat, perhaps gnawing away at bloodied meat, tearing it from the bone, is not helpful in comprehending these words of Jesus. I want to submit my own rendition of a vision that might help man understand the meaning intended by

Jesus when He instituted the sacrament of Holy Communion.

When you or someone else speaks the words of consecration over bread and wine, a miracle occurs. I have found it helpful to visualize that miracle this way. When you actually swallow the concentrated bread or wine imagine God transforming Himself into a vapor. Within seconds that vapor covers every cell in your body from every brain cell all the way down to every single cell of blood, water, bone, muscle or tissue. That Vapor is Divine, it is actually God Himself. And He is blessing you by His divine presence in every cell in your body, covering each of those millions of cells with His very own Divine Presence. As you speak to God during the few minutes after Communion ask Him to heal whatever in your body, or the body of anyone else you know, with His Divine healing. The vapor slowly fades and after about 15 minutes it is completely dissolved.

Chapter Four

Divine Healing

"I don't know what the future may hold, but I know who holds the future." Ralph Abernathy

"The forces that are for you are greater than those that are against you." Joel Osteen

"Hope is praying for rain, but faith is bringing an umbrella." Unknown

"Once you choose hope, anything's possible." Christopher Reeve

"Most folks are as happy as they make up their minds to be." Abraham Lincoln. There are many men and women who have experienced miraculous and unexplainable cures, such as the utter disappearance of cancerous tumors and other unexplainable praenomina when they prayed for those things while receiving Holy Communion. One of the key scriptures related to Divine Healing comes from Isaiah 53:5, ""But He was wounded by our transgressions. He was *bruised by ou inequities.*

The Chastisement for our peace was upon Him. And by His stripes we are healed. NKJV The Catholics meanwhile recognized that a major miracle had occurred, but, as Catholics tend to do, they took the word of God, clearly expressed in the Bible, and staffed that word through the Vatican. The word of God when augmented by the word of some Pope, is no longer the word of God, but has become the not at all significant words of some Pope or Vatican Officials. I asked my former Pastor, Dr. Jimmy Nelson, "To whom was Jesus speaking at that Last Supper?" His answer was simple and direct. He simply said, To His Church. When God said: Do this in remembrance of me?" he was speaking to every believer. For a Pope to take that message and defile it by saying that the only people who could consecrate, or, as the Catholics call it, preform the transubstantiation, are men who have graduated from a Catholic Seminary and have been ordained by a high official of the Catholic Church. That is nothing at all like what Jesus said or meant when He instituted the power of consecration of bread and wine into His very own body and blood. Saying that only an educated and ordained Catholic Priest possess the power to do what God Himself said, any and all members of His Church, could and should do, is a ridiculous absurdity.

Please focus now on the last few words of a significant Bible verse concerning the power of Jesus to heal, in Isaiah 53:5, ""And by His stripes we are healed." If Jesus was condemned to be beaten with a brutal 20 lashes, each lash of the whip must have ripped and torn the skin off His precious back. Now, realize that the Egyptians worshipped cats, and instigated the tale that cats have nine lives. It was probably the Egyptians who designed a cruel instrument of torture, which contained not just a single lash, but nine lashes, commonly referred to as the "Cat of nine tails." We believe that Jesus was beaten with a cat of nine tails whip, and therefore received not just 20 lashes, but 20 times nine or 180 lashes. Some have criticized Mel Gibson for the brutality he included in the Movie He made on the crucifixion.

Actually audiences would not and could not have tolerated seeing what Jesus actually looked like following his scourging at the pillar. Great swatches of His skin had been sliced and cut open, and were left hanging from His body. Please understand this, dear reader, those bloodied and dead flaps of skin hanging from the back of Jesus were part of the price He paid for each of us so that we might be forgiven, and welcomed into fellowship with the God of Gods, the one true God, Jesus Christ. Those stripes on His back, dear readers, are just a small part of what Jesus paid for your, and for my own, and for every sinner's freedom.

Chapter Five

Special Intentions

"Winners aren't people who never fail, but people who never quit" Unknown

"I have not failed. I've just found 10,000 ways that won't work." Thomas Edison

"You can't go back and change the beginning, but you can start where you are and change the ending" C.S. Lewis

A man once told a Buddha, "I want happiness. The Buddha replied, "remove the word, "I." that is ego." "Then remove "want," that's desire. And now all you have left is happiness." Unknown

"It's never too late to be what you might have been." George Eliot

Any time you receive Holy Communion, it is both possible and appropriate to ask God, just before receiving Communion, to accept that Communion for a special intention. I. for example, have a dear friend who is fighting a daily battle in the final stages with a vicious Cancer. Just before I receive Communion I ask God to bless that particular communion for the intention of alleviating some of that woman's discomfort, and if it be God's will, to restore her health.

Now, I ask you to concentrate for just a few seconds on what actually occurs when a Believer receives Hold Communion. God and man are about to be intimately connected for a brief part of a day. The

Catholics teach that the intimate effects of Holy Communion linger for about 15 minutes, and after that, the bread has been absorbed by and completely dissolved by the human body. That sounds about right to me, and I believe that teaching is probably accurate. During that 15-minute period of intimacy, man and Jesus Christ, man's acknowledged God, will be as intimate as it is possible for two beings to come together in a union. The very word," Communion" communicates what occurs during the miracle of Holy Communion. During a Communion ceremony, man is able to **COMM** into **UNION** with Jesus Christ, with God Almighty. That is such a miraculous occurrence, and such a beautiful gift God himself delivered to man and to mankind. Man has absolutely no chance of ascending anywhere close to the heavenly level of God's domain, so, in order for man to be in a union with God

Himself, God must come down close to man's level. Through the miracle of Holy Communion, man requests a brief time with God, and because God does indeed show up, whenever He is called though Holy Communion, then God, for that brief 15 minutes, becomes as intimate as it is possible to become, with the man or woman who called out to Him through Holy Communion.

Because man is incapable and so terribly inadequate at discussing God-things with God, God, in His kindness and His divine mercy, focuses on the affairs of the man or woman who called out to Him. Whatever is on your mind is therefore important to God. If the thoughts which are dominant in your mind, during that particular communion, and if you are concentrating on something as trivial to God, as who will win a game played by the Dallas

Cowboys, or the Mudville High School Baseball team, then that is acceptable to God, because He is in your life for an intimate conversation with you. Whatever you want to talk with God about is okay, because it's your 15 minutes. You just take it and use it for whatever you think is important. The thing to remember is it's your 15 minutes with God, so you are free to use it any way you choose.

Chapter Six

Your Adversary, The Devil

"Be sober, be vigilant, because your adversary the Devil, as a roaring lion, walketh about seeking whom to devour;" 1 Peter 6:8

"For wherever God builds a church, there the Devil would also build a chapel." Martin Luther

"Hell is the highest reward the Devil can offer you for being a servant of his." Billy Sunday

There is a murderer at large and he was spotted close to your home. I know for a fact that he knows your name and has been targeting you. His name is Satan, the Devil, and he is a cunning and ruthless adversary. It was no exaggeration when Peter wrote of Him, "He walketh about, as a roaring lion, seeking whom to devour." He is so powerful that you cannot defeat him without help. That help must come from the One Supreme Being, who has demonstrated the capability to handle the Devil. That, of course, is Jesus Christ, who expelled the Devil and all of his followers, and cast them down to a dark earth, where they remain today.

Satan, or as He is sometimes called, "Lucifer, Beliar, Beelzebul, or Beelizeebub" is real. As Pope Francis said, "We should not talk of the devil as myth, a representation, a symbol, a figure of speech or an idea "lest we let our guard down." Taken from the website at www.theconversation.com/friday-essay-Satan-is-back-again-the-Devil-in-5-dark-details-162859

Paul wrote in Ephesians 6:11,"…to put on the full armor of God so that you may be able to stand against the wiles of the Devil." We were also warned against the Devil by Isidore, Bishop of Seville, "The foolery of the magic arts held sway over the entire world for many centuries through the instructions of evil angels. All of these things are to be avoided by a Christian, and are entirely repudiated and condemned." This information was also taken from www.theconversation.com at the address above. Please recognize the fact that so-called "dabbling" with the tools used in Satanic practices is dangerous and should be avoided. These are not toys, and an intelligent person will avoid all contact with Satanically linked tools such as tea leaf reading, horoscopes, seances, tarot cards or ouija boards. Understand and appreciate that the Devil is very real and should not be trivialized or used for entertainment purposes.

www.ingramcontent.com/pod-product-compliance
Lightning Source LLC
LaVergne TN
LVHW040203080526
838202LV00042B/3305